MW00881089

Hillary Clinton: Ground-Breaking Politician

by Jeanne Marie Ford

MG (4-8)
ATOS 5.1
0.5 pts
Non-Fiction

193374 EN

Hillary Clinton
GROUND-BREAKING POLITICIAN

BY JEANNE MARIE FORD

Published by The Child's World®
1980 Lookout Drive • Mankato, MN 56003-1705
800-599-READ • www.childsworld.com

Photographs ©: Andrew Harnik/AP Images, cover, 1; Evan El-Amin/Shutterstock
Images, 5; Joseph Sohm/Shutterstock Images, 6, 20; Danny Johnston/AP Images, 9;
Luc Novovitch/Reuters/Newscom, 10; Toby Talbot/AP Images, 13; Jim McKnight/AP
Images, 14; Steve Marcus/Reuters/Newscom, 16; Saul Loeb/AP Images, 18

ISBN 9781503823983
LCCN 2017944735

Printed in the United States of America
PA02362

ABOUT THE AUTHOR

Jeanne Marie Ford is an Emmy-winning TV scriptwriter and holds an MFA
in Writing for Children from Vermont College. She has written numerous
children's books and articles and also teaches college English. She lives in
Maryland with her husband and two children.

TABLE OF
CONTENTS

FAST FACTS

Full Name

- Hillary Diane Rodham Clinton

Birthdate

- October 26, 1947, in Chicago, Illinois

Husband

- President William Jefferson Clinton

Children

- Chelsea Clinton

Years in White House

- 1993–2001

Accomplishments

- Won a Grammy Award in 1997 for the audio recording of her book *It Takes a Village.*

- Became the first female U.S. senator from New York and first First Lady to win elective office.

- Served as secretary of state under President Barack Obama.

- Selected as first female presidential **nominee** of a major U.S. political party.

Chapter 1

HILLARY RODHAM

Hugh Rodham was dying. His daughter, Hillary, squeezed his hand. For days, she sat beside him as the monitors beeped and whirred.

Hillary Clinton had been First Lady for only nine weeks when her father had a stroke. When she finally had to leave his bedside to give a speech, she had not had time to write it. She had no idea what she was going to say.

Fourteen thousand people came to the University of Texas at Austin to hear her. She spoke powerfully about the human spirit and the importance of caring for one another. When she had finished, even the **Secret Service** agents were in tears.

◀ Hillary Clinton was a huge component in helping Bill Clinton win the presidency in 1992.

The next day, Hillary's father died. In high school, Hillary was a Republican. When she was accepted at Wellesley College, a teacher told Hillary she would become a Democrat. Hillary was certain he would be wrong.

But by the time she graduated from Wellesley, Hillary had been exposed to a whole new world. On a bright May day, Hillary became the first student ever to give Wellesley's graduation speech.

Hillary went on to attend Yale Law School. One day in the student lounge, Hillary noticed a tall, curly-haired young man. His name was Bill Clinton. A few days later, Hillary introduced herself. They started dating. After a few years, Bill and Hillary moved to Arkansas. They got married in the sunny living room of their home on October 11, 1975.

In 1978, Hillary became First Lady of Arkansas when Bill was elected governor. The next year, she was named the first female partner at her law firm. Their daughter, Chelsea Clinton, was born soon afterward.

After his fifth term as Arkansas governor, Bill decided to run for president of the United States. Following a long and hard **campaign** in 1992, Hillary proudly voted for her husband. He became the 42nd president.

▲ As First Lady of Arkansas, Hillary began her efforts for many causes, such as helping increase education standards in 1983.

Chapter 2

FIRST LADY

At the Smithsonian's American History Museum, Hillary walked slowly through the First Ladies Exhibit. She looked at Barbara Bush's camouflage jacket among the glittering ball gowns and thought about the roles of First Ladies throughout history. She wondered what hers would be.

Hillary's passion had always been for helping children. She expected to continue that work in the White House. But the American people had never had a First Lady with her own career. When Hillary talked about having a job instead of "staying at home to make cookies and serve tea," she received hundreds of angry letters.[1]

◄ Hillary became a part of the First Ladies exhibit when she donated the gown she wore to Bill's inauguration in 1993.

Only a few weeks before her father's stroke, Bill had asked Hillary to lead an effort to improve the health care system. Hugh Rodham's illness helped her understand what changes needed to be made.

Despite thousands of hours of hard work, Hillary's health care plan never received a vote in Congress. But she persisted. She worked with both political parties to provide better health care to poor children.

Hillary and Chelsea also traveled the world to work for more rights for women and children. In a Mongolian tent, Hillary drank fermented milk with a local family. In Uganda, she saw the aftermath of horrors faced by women who had lived through the Rwandan war.

By the end of Bill's second term, the Clintons' marriage was in trouble. **Scandals** involving money and personal relationships followed Bill throughout his presidency. He was eventually **impeached** by the House of Representatives, although the Senate did not **convict** him. Hillary relied on her Christian faith to carry her through such hard times.

▲ Hillary spoke many times about her health care bill.

But before the end of Bill's second term, the Democratic Party asked Hillary to run for office. The offer was for a U.S. Senate seat representing New York State. She accepted the challenge.

GORE
LIEBERMAN
HILLARY
VOTE
NOVEMBER 7
GORE
LIEBERMAN
HILLARY
VOTE

Chapter 3

SENATOR CLINTON

Balloons and confetti rained down on Hillary as she stood in a New York City ballroom in November 2000. She thanked the crowd for electing her the first female senator from New York. Bill and Chelsea stood by her side.

Months later, lower Manhattan erupted in flames as two planes struck the World Trade Center. Hillary stood amid the rubble and smoke with Mayor Rudy Giuliani, her former political rival. She fought hard for government money to rebuild New York and for first responders who got sick from working at Ground Zero. In 2006, New Yorkers elected her to a second term in a **landslide**.

◄ Chelsea Clinton was often by her mother's side on the 2000 campaign trail.

Hillary decided to run for president in the 2008 election. She was expected to win the Democratic **nomination** but fell behind Senator Barack Obama of Illinois. On the election trail in New Hampshire, she gave a moving speech. "Some people think elections are a game," she said. "But," she declared, "it's about our country. It's about our kids' future. It's about all of us together."[2]

"We're stronger when every family in every community knows they're not on their own, because we're all in this together. It really does 'take a village'—to raise a child and to build a stronger future for us all."[3]

— Hillary Clinton, June 2016

◀ During her campaign for the 2008 presidential election, Hillary had to debate Senator Barack Obama several times.

Chapter 4

MADAM SECRETARY

In June 2008, a van with tinted windows whisked Hillary to a secret meeting with the Democratic presidential nominee, Barack Obama. During the **primary** race, they had been bitter enemies. However, they shared many ideas about the future of the country. Hillary decided to offer Obama her support. After he was elected, he asked her to be secretary of state. She accepted.

Over the next four years, Secretary Clinton visited 112 countries and continued to work for human rights around the world. While she had many accomplishments, some people blamed her when four Americans were killed in Benghazi, Libya. Her use of a private e-mail server was also criticized, but she was never convicted of any crime.

◄ The job of secretary of state took Hillary all around the world. Here she is in Myanmar in 2011.

▲ Many people often spoke on Hillary's behalf, such as fellow First Lady Michelle Obama.

In 2016, Hillary ran for president again. This time, she won the Democratic nomination. She became the first female nominee for a major political party. Hillary narrowly lost the election to Donald Trump.

A few days later, Hillary gave a speech at a fund-raiser. "I will admit coming here wasn't the easiest thing," she said. "There have been a few times this past week where all I wanted to do was curl up with a good book, or our dogs, and never leave the house again."

But, she said, it was important to "believe in our country, fight for our values, and never give up."[4] Hillary Clinton would keep on fighting. She would never give up.

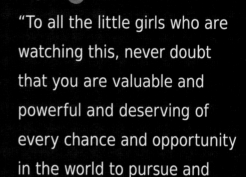

"To all the little girls who are watching this, never doubt that you are valuable and powerful and deserving of every chance and opportunity in the world to pursue and achieve your own dreams."[5]

— Hillary Clinton, November 2016

THINK ABOUT IT

- The First Lady is not an elected official. What kind of power should she have in the White House?
- The wife of a president is called the First Lady. If a president's spouse is male, what would his title be?
- How might life in the United States be different with a female president?

GLOSSARY

campaign (kam-PAYN): In politics, a campaign is an organized effort to get a candidate elected. Hillary Clinton helped on her husband Bill's presidential campaign.

convict (kun-VIKT): To convict is to find someone guilty of a crime. Hillary Clinton stood by her husband's side while the House of Representatives voted to convict him.

impeached (im-PEECHT): Presidents are impeached when they are charged of wrongdoing. Bill Clinton was impeached based on evidence that he had lied under oath.

landslide (LAND-slide): A candidate who wins an election by a large number of votes is said to win in a landslide. Hillary Clinton was reelected to the U.S. Senate in a landslide.

nomination (nah-min-AY-shun): A nomination is when someone is appointed for office. Hillary lost the 2008 Democratic nomination to Barack Obama.

nominee (nah-muh-NEE): A nominee is a person who is nominated for a position or award. Hillary Clinton was the first female Democratic presidential nominee.

primary (PRYE-mayr-ee): A primary (first) election selects a party's nominees for the general election. Barack Obama and Hillary Clinton were running against each other in the 2008 primary.

scandals (SKAN-duls): Scandals are events that the public believes may involve wrongdoing. The Clintons dealt with many scandals during Bill's years as president.

Secret Service (SEE-krit SUR-viss): The Secret Service are special agents who work for the government. Hillary Clinton's speech after her father died made the Secret Service members tear up.

SOURCE NOTES

1. Gwen Ifill. "The 1992 Campaign; Hillary Clinton Defends Her Conduct in Law Firm." *New York Times*. New York Times Company, 17 Mar. 1992. Web. 31 May 2017.

2. Karen Breslau. "Hillary Clinton's Emotional Moment." *Newsweek*. Newsweek, 6 Jan. 2008. Web. 31 May 2017.

3. Hillary Clinton. "Remarks on Securing the Democratic Nomination." *HillaryClinton.com*. Hillary for America, 1 July 2016. Web. 31 May 2017.

4. Rebecca Savransky and Judy Kurtz. "Clinton: 'All I Wanted to Do Was Just to Curl Up' This Past Week." *The Hill*. Capitol Hill Publishing, 11 Nov. 2016. Web. 31 May 2017.

5. "Hillary Clinton Biography." *Biography*. A&E Television Networks, 16 Dec. 2016. Web. 10 Apr. 2017.

TO LEARN MORE

Books

Alexander, Heather. *Who Is Hillary Clinton?* New York, NY: Grosset & Dunlap, 2016.

Clinton, Chelsea. *It's Your World: Get Informed, Get Inspired & Get Going!* New York, NY: Philomel Books, 2015.

Doak, Robin S. *Hillary Clinton.* New York, NY: Children's Press, 2013.

Web Sites

Visit our Web site for links about Hillary Clinton:

childsworld.com/links

Note to Parents, Teachers, and Librarians: We routinely verify our Web links to make sure they are safe and active sites. So encourage your readers to check them out!

INDEX